THEY LIED TO US

True Stories about
the damaging effects of abortion
told by
the women who survived them

Victoria Laktash

WORLDCOMM®
a division of Creativity, Inc.

ISBN: 1-466323-41-8
ISBN-13:   9781466323414

CONTENTS

Preface 6

A Message from the Author 8

Close to Mommy's Heart 9

Victoria 10

Alexandra 17

Tammy 23

Pat 28

Sabrina 32

Ingrid 38

Lindsay & Joe 44

Trina 52

Rachel 60

About the Author 64

Victoria with her daughters: Tawni, Kolby, Victoria, Kendra, Teryn

Acknowledgements Page

George - your unconditional love and support simply amaze me. You truly are my best friend. I love you.

My four daughters, Teryn, Tawni, Kendra and Kolby - You are four of the best decisions I've ever made in my life. I am blessed to be your mother and sharing all of your lives with you. You are my greatest achievements in life and I couldn't be more proud of each one of you. I love you "high as the sky, deep as the sea, and all the air that's in between."

Salem - My precious Lil Pooks. Your Mimi could not imagine her life without you in it. You make my heart full. I love being your grandmother.

Trudy - you continue to inspire me, even from Heaven. I miss you terribly and will love you always.

Granny - "my little Granny". I love you more than words.

Mom and Dad - thanks for deciding to have me.

Jim, Val, Erica and Hannah- you're great friends, but more like family. I love you all!

Brenda - I'm blessed to have a sister with your wisdom.

To Carolyn Rice and Trina Pitts, Post-Abortion Counselors - without your counseling, I would never have recovered from my decision of abortion. Thank you for guiding me through my healing.

To my precious friends for their love and support - Annette Lynch, Misty Shell, Judy Heaton, Andrea Perez, Larissa Ortiz, Shannon Creamer, Mackenzie Shunko, Keri Pomarolli-McGehee, Marcie Hodges, Michelle Lee, Ann and Alan Fortner. I am blessed to know each one of you.

The Ambassador's Speakers Group: Gloria Leyda, Wes Yoder, Maria Yates & Christine Hawley - thank you so much for your editing expertise! You guys are wonderful to work with and I'm proud to call you friends.

To my children who reside in Heaven - through my own abortion or miscarriages, your residency is now with God. I long for the day I meet each one of you, but will continue my work until I do.

To the women who took part in this book - thank you for sharing your greatest pain and secret with the world. You will always be dear to my heart.

Most importantly, I want to thank God and Savior Jesus Christ. In my life, You have witnessed the great joy and pain I've been through and You've never left me. Each of my experiences, good or bad, has taught me something of great value. I thank You, my Heavenly Father, for guiding me in taking one of the most personal and painful experiences of my life and creating something wonderful from them. May You receive all the glory, honor and praise for anything that I do. I absolutely adore You and I'm forever grateful to finally realize how much I need you.

Preface

This is a book about a very sensitive subject. Daily, much debate surrounds it. It is about abortion and the deep scars that it leaves on those affected by it. These stories are from the women who've experienced and survived them. Many types of women are represented here. Young, old, rich and poor, some are educated and some are not.

Despite their differences, each shares a common goal. They are desperate for others to hear and know the truth about how the decision to abort changed their lives. Our hope and prayer is that these stories will find their way into the hands of women contemplating abortion. We want them to hear from women who've walked where they may be choosing to go.

Although the stories were written by women and for women, it is not the intention that men be excluded from reading them. We understand that men too have been greatly affected by the atrocities of abortion. At times it's a hard read, but a necessary one. This is not only a book about pain, but also a book about healing.

It will not be popular among many and will make others uncomfortable. Although it is not the intention to offend, I know that won't be possible. I'm willing to take the risks associated with this project, as I believe with all of my heart, the truth must be told from the true experts, those who've lived it. Unfortunately, there will be those who don't want to know this truth.

Millions of people from all walks of life have been affected by abortion. Not only directly, but indirectly. Maybe you're one of them. Or maybe you've never experienced the circumstances of those you'll read about. My prayer is that you never have or that you never will be.

It's time to speak out about the other side of abortion that no one wants to talk about. The real truth of how it has and does affect the women who've chosen it. Abortion is not the quick, easy solution that the pro-choice advocates would have you believe. There is a great price to pay for the men and women who make such a choice. But few, if any, until now, have spoken out about what it cost them.

The women represented in this book are passionate about getting their stories told. They want to prevent other women from possibly enduring the pain and suffering they've had to live with, some for as many as thirty-six years.

Every story in this book is true. Some women have chosen to remain anonymous, but nothing from their actual story has been changed.

If you or someone you love is struggling from a past abortion, our hope is that the stories found in this book will help you realize that you're not alone. There is help available to you.

If you're courageous enough, no matter what your stand on abortion, I challenge you to read this book. It could change your life. I warn you, it could even change your mind.

A Message from the Author

I, along with many others, am convinced that the rise in depression, along with the various prescribed anti-depressant drugs have reached proportionate levels due to abortion. As I have met, interviewed and counseled post-abortive women, I've found that they have many things in common. Some of the greatest of these are depression, low self-esteem and fear. One of the greatest fears these women share is never being able to have another child or possibly losing one of their living children. Some women don't understand why they're experiencing many of the emotional and/or physical problems that have plagued them for years. Others aren't realizing until years later that thoughts of suicide, guilt and anger could be coming from a past abortion.

With many of the women that I've interviewed, I am the first person they've shared their "secret" with. There is so much guilt and shame associated with abortion that it takes every ounce of courage they have to say, "I've had an abortion". As I've listened to their heart wrenching stories and heard their cries for help, I've been more determined than ever to write this book.

As women are sharing their abortion experiences with me, I sense a newfound "freedom" in their attitudes. Just being able to talk about it with someone helps tremendously. It also helps to start them on their road to recovery. Each woman is convinced that she is the only one suffering from her decision to abort.

Getting to know these wonderful women has been one of the greatest highlights of my life. I treasure each one and consider them my friends. We have rejoiced together as we have embarked on this journey to complete healing and forgiveness.

I have been both privileged and honored that these precious people would share their hearts and deepest secrets with me. I can and do empathize with each and every one of them. I know where they're coming from. I understand their pain and suffering. I've experienced years of my own. This book is very personal to me. You see, the first story you're about to read is mine.

A Baby's Prayer
By Kathy Trocolli

I can hear her talking with a friend
I think it's all about me
Oh, how she can't have a baby now
My mommy doesn't see
That I feel her breathe
I know her voice
Her blood is flows through my heart
God, you know my greatest wish is that
We'd never be apart

But, if I should die before I wake
I pray her soul You'll keep
Forgive her, Lord, she doesn't know
That You gave life to me

Do I really have to say good-bye
Don't want this time to be through
God, please tell her that I love her, Lord
And that You love her too

Cause if I should die before I wake
I pray her soul You'll keep
Forgive her, Lord, she doesn't know
That You gave life to me

On the days when she may think of me
Please comfort her with the truth
That the angels hold me safe and sound
Cause I'm in Heaven with You, I'm in Heaven with You

Victoria

In 1986, after five-and-a-half years of marriage, my husband left me alone to raise two young daughters. My oldest daughter was three, my youngest a mere nine months old. This wasn't supposed to happen. I believed that my marriage would last forever. I was twenty-one years old. The last thing I wanted for my daughters was to experience the trauma that I had from my own parent's divorce. To say that I was devastated would be an understatement.

When you suddenly find yourself faced with being a single mother, your perspective on life and yourself changes drastically. Feelings of inadequacy plagued my every thought.

I was at the lowest point in my life and desperate for someone to love me again. Sometimes we need to be careful what we wish for. Eight months after my husband left, I met the man that I believed was the best thing that ever happened to me. I believed he would love me forever. I fell madly in love with him and he knew it. He noticed my vulnerability right away and took every advantage of it that he could. I would have given up my life for him.

Four months into our relationship, I found out I was pregnant. Devastated, I knew the last thing that I needed at this point in my life was another child. Yet part of me was excited about the idea of having his baby. When I told him about the pregnancy, he was very calm and suggested right away that I have an abortion. He actually insisted. He convinced me that we could have children later on, but not now. I believed him when he said it was for the best.

I had always looked down on women who'd had abortions. It would make me angry when women used abortion as a form of birth control. Now here I was faced with the same decision they had faced. I now convinced myself that it wasn't a big deal after all. I searched the yellow pages and easily found the number to the local abortion clinic in the town where I lived. I telephoned the clinic and was told by the clinic that because I was so early in my pregnancy, I wasn't carrying a "real" baby. Her exact words were, "it's just a blob of cells, 'it' hasn't formed into a human being yet."

The woman on the other end insisted that I have the "procedure" performed right away, the sooner, the better. She always referred to it as the "procedure," never mentioning the word abortion. She said I was only "terminating a pregnancy."

She instructed me to bring cash only to my visit. Checks or credit cards were not accepted. I made an appointment for that Saturday morning at 9:30 A.M. My boyfriend would be out of town so I'd have to drive myself. I couldn't ask anyone to take me because, God forbid, I couldn't tell anyone about the mess I'd gotten myself into. What would they think of me? Funny. If I was so convinced that this was OK, why should I care what others would think? I did care. This would have been called a clue.

On Saturday morning, the babysitter for my two young daughters arrived. I told her that I would be doing some shopping for a few hours. I remember looking at my daughters, playing happily on the floor. I wondered, "If they only knew what I'm about to do, what would they think of me?"

The drive was a long one even though it was only fifteen minutes away. I kept trying to think of other things. The groceries I needed to buy, the shoes that the girls' needed. At one time as I drove to the clinic, I placed my hand over my stomach and begged for forgiveness for what I was about to do, still convinced I was doing the right thing. Still conveniently convincing myself that "it" wasn't a real baby anyway. I was only terminating a pregnancy, right? That's what that caring, sympathetic woman on the other end of the phone had said. Why would she lie to me?

When I arrived, I pulled into the parking lot and sat in my car for a moment. I began taking deep, long breaths. It was almost my appointment time and I didn't want to be late.

I'd heard about picketers before, but this must have been their day off. No one was there to talk some sense into me about what I was about to do. I don't know that it would have mattered, but for years it was my crutch. It's always easier to blame others rather than accept responsibility our selves. What a cowardly society in which we live.

As I rode the elevator, I could hear my heart beating. I thought it would explode through my chest. There were other people getting off on different floors. I wondered if they knew. My hands were sweaty and I was very nervous.

When I reached my floor, I found the door to the clinic and walked in. I announced that I'd arrived to the receptionist and sat in the lobby with about ten other women. The room was packed. No one was looking around, just kind of staring at the floor. The room was very still, as we waited our turn.

When my fictitious name was called, I quickly got up and went into the first of three rooms. This was the office of the cashier. She sat me down, shut the door and matter-of-factly asked, "Do you have your money with you?" I nodded. "I need the full $350.00, cash only, as I told you over the phone. Remember, if you change your mind while you're on the table, you don't get your money back. There are no refunds here. Do you understand this?" I nodded again.

I said, "Are you sure this is OK?"

She asked me, "How far along are you again?"

I answered, "I think four weeks."

She then said, "Well, if the doctor does determine that you're a lot farther along, it will cost you more money."

I asked again, "Should I really do this?" She seemed nervous. Maybe I was about to change my mind and she wouldn't make her "quota" for the day.

I guess she wanted to reassure me when she said, "Look, when you leave this place, never think of this day again. Just forget about it. You'll be fine and you can always have more babies later. You're too early in your pregnancy to even think of this as a real pregnancy, let alone a real baby. Remember and never forget, we're only terminating a pregnancy." There it was again, that lie.

It was obvious she'd done this before. Her "speech" was so rehearsed. I handed her my money and was then taken into the next waiting area where I was told to undress and put a hospital like gown on. I was given a muscle relaxer and a cup of water. They asked me not to speak to any of the other women. It might be too uncomfortable for them. So, along with several others, I took my medicine and waited to be called.

We were all sharing the same fate, yet none of us could even look at one another. We were too ashamed and embarrassed. You could sense it in the atmosphere. Finally, it was my turn. When my name was called, I was taken into the next room, my final destination. If I was going to change my mind, now was the time to do it.

I was in a state of shock. I felt like I was having an out of body experience. Like I was viewing a horror movie and I was the star. As I walked down the hallway, I felt a strong urge to turn around and run. I wanted to scream, "No! I've changed my mind!" I heard the words in my head, even in my heart! But the words wouldn't come. I couldn't breathe, let alone speak. I was terrified that if I told them I wanted out of there, they'd get mad at me! Imagine that! I was getting ready to abort my child and I was worried about what they would think!

When the doctor came in, there were no formal introductions. The first words he spoke to me were, "Slide down and place your feet in the stirrups." The next thing I heard was the sound of a loud machine, like a broken vacuum. The sound was deafening. The nurse explained it was all part of the "procedure." There was that word again.

I remember how cold the doctor's hands were. His attitude was even colder. It didn't take long for me to realize that I meant nothing to him. I was only a means to his livelihood.

After what seemed like forever, but in reality was only a few minutes, it was over. My problem had been solved, or so I thought. As the doctor started to leave the room, I called out to him. I needed to know if it was a boy or girl. I wanted to know how far along I was. Could he please reassure me that it wasn't a "real" baby? I noticed that he rolled his eyes at me. He seemed irritated that I would dare speak to him.

Didn't I know he had lots of work to do, many rooms to visit? He acted like I didn't have any right to ask anything. Maybe he was right, but he did answer. He said, "You're about four to six weeks and no, of course I can't tell you what it is. It was too early to tell." And with that, he was gone. I never saw him again, except in my nightmares.

The nurse walked me to the "recovery room" where I was placed on a cot with the others. The room was full. I was given two Tylenol and told to lie down. She said when I felt like getting up and leaving, I could dress and go. She suggested I stay for at least an hour. Five minutes passed and I quickly got myself dressed. I had to get out of there. Now! With tears streaming down my face, I ran as fast as I could to the elevator and then to my car.

I didn't think I would make it home safely, but I did. I could barely see the road. I was crying so hard. I knew right away that I'd made a mistake. But it was too late! There was no way to change what I'd done! My baby was gone!

When I got home, I thanked and paid the babysitter. She didn't question my condition. I'm sure she was quite confused as to why I was so upset from shopping! Even my young daughters were confused at my state of mind. They didn't understand why mommy was so sad. I didn't understand either, I mean isn't this what I wanted? I laid in my bed the rest of the day. I thought I was going to drown. I wanted to die. I prayed that I would bleed to death.

There was no one for me to talk to because I couldn't tell anyone. I was so ashamed. I wanted my mother so bad, but I knew I couldn't tell her. She'd always thought of me as the "good daughter." She loved her grandchildren very much and I had just killed one of them.

My boyfriend came over that evening. He was always good at saying the right things and he held me as I cried throughout the night. Over and over he promised we would have children one day. Along with the others involved in my abortion, he lied. Our relationship ended not long afterwards. I didn't know it at the time, but statistics show that this is what happens to nine out of ten relationships where an abortion occurs.

Staying together is just too painful a reminder of what you did. It would make sense to me that he lost respect for me after the abortion. And I'm sure I never felt the same about him either. What kind of man insists that you kill his flesh and blood? Even though he was insistent about my having one, I'm sure he never looked at me the same afterwards. So, I had an abortion to keep him, but not only did I lose him, I lost my baby and my self-respect also. Nothing felt the same to me after that day. Not for a long, long time.

For fifteen years, I have lived with the shame and guilt of my abortion. It has kept me from bonding with friends and robbed me of my self-esteem. Throughout all of these years, to be happy made me feel tremendous guilt. I have never felt that I've deserved anything good in my life. In my punishment, I never allowed myself to experience true joy. Any blessing that had come after my abortion, I couldn't enjoy to the fullest. I've been convinced I didn't deserve any of them.

Anxiety attacks, depression, guilt and shame were just a few of the repercussions of my decision to abort. When I finally came to the realization that these traits stemmed from my abortion experience, it was then that I was able to get the help I needed. I thank God everyday for healing me, forgiving me and most of all helping me to forgive myself and the others who took part in my abortion.

For all of these years, I have hated my boyfriend, the doctor, the clinic workers and even the pro-lifers for what I did. I wondered where they were on that Saturday morning. Why weren't they there screaming at me, begging me not to go in. I've even hated and blamed God for what I'd done.

Through my healing process, I've learned to accept responsibility for what I did. I can no longer live in the denial that my child wasn't real or that what I did was someone else's fault. I know that God was there that day. He was grieving for what He knew was going to cost me years of pain and suffering. Because of His grace and mercy, I truly feel forgiven and set free.

Abortion is not the quick, easy solution as some have been made to believe. It is an agonizing, life altering choice that we, post-abortive women, are forced to live with for the rest of our lives. The cost that I've paid and will pay for my decision to abort was a greater price than I would have ever paid had I given birth to my child. I don't argue that it would have been extremely difficult to be a single mother of three small children. But, there were other options. Even adoption would have been a better choice. My mentality was "How can I carry a baby and then give it up for adoption? No way, I'll just abort instead". How crazy is that?

I would give anything to know that I had a child who was alive and that someday would search for me, her biological mother. But that day will never come for me because my child is gone. I never gave my child a chance to search for me. My child will never ring my phone or knock on my door. Abortion was too permanent a solution. You can never take it back. If I knew then what I know now, abortion would have never been a part of my life. I took the coward's way out.

Had the "experts" explained to me that in the future I could experience the levels of fear, rejection, pain and depression as a result of my abortion experience, would things have been different for me? Would I have made a different decision? Maybe and maybe not, but I should have been given that chance. To know the whole truth about what this decision could cost me. The system lied and betrayed me by even suggesting that I could forget about it and never think of it again. It's not right that our government allows such an atrocity to take place every day in this country without laws being enforced that women are told of some of the repercussions of a decision to abort.

Even cigarette boxes carry, by law, a surgeon general's warning that smoking can be hazardous to your health. Yet, women choose abortion every day, never being told the risks involved.

For years, I've had to live with the consequences of the decision I made to take life instead of give it. I have had to deal with theses consequences and it has, at times, been very difficult. I will never forget what happened that day. Even though I have experienced and felt God's love and forgiveness, I will always live with the regret of what I did.

Like a reformed alcoholic still craves the drink, I will always long to hold the child I never knew. My comfort comes in knowing that one day in Heaven, that longing will be fulfilled.

Alexandra

When I was a freshman in high school, I started dating the young man that I thought could be "the one." I'll call him Greg. Greg and I were high school sweethearts all throughout high school and we were in love! About a year into the relationship, we decided to become sexually involved. I couldn't ask my mother for any type of birth control so we thought we would be "safe" using the withdrawal method. There were a couple of times that we took our chances, but we never worried about it.

I'd always planned on going to college. My dad wouldn't have it any other way. Greg would be staying back home, but we had it all planned. We would continue to see each other on weekends as often as possible. Although we were still a couple, I sensed deep changes taking place in our relationship and how we felt about each other. We were growing more and more distant from one another. I think he resented my going to college because he couldn't afford to.

Ignoring my strong feelings, I stayed in the relationship and we continued to have sex. We were still practicing the withdrawal method for birth control and didn't see any reason to change it.

Two weeks before I was to leave for college, I discovered I was pregnant. I was floored! What was I supposed to do now? I couldn't tell my parents! I couldn't let my dad down. Ever since I'd found out I was accepted into college, he treated me differently. According to him, I'd finally done something right.

Growing up, I'd always felt I had to work for my father's love and approval. I had finally done something right in his eyes and there was no way some pregnancy was going to ruin that for me! I couldn't have a baby now! I had to go to college! This was my dream! If I was going to make something out of my life, I knew I had to have an education.

I explained all of this to Greg. I told him there was no way I was having a baby at this time in my life. He didn't argue. It made sense to him.

We knew what we had to do and we made the decision to do it. We determined the best way to keep our secret from being revealed was to go about our lives as planned. I would leave for college as scheduled and Greg would pick me up in two weeks, bring me home and we'd take care of our problem. We made an appointment to have an abortion and that was that. We didn't discuss it again.

When I arrived at college, I tried to keep myself busy so I would be too occupied to think about my condition over the next two weeks. Within days, I began having migraine headaches. I'd never had them before. The pain was so severe that I visited the emergency room several times. The doctors ran tests on me and found nothing to support why I was having these headaches. My mom was a great source of encouragement and support. She was very worried about me.

Two weeks went by and Greg came to pick me up. We drove three hours home in silence. Greg wouldn't talk to me. I noticed that he couldn't even look at me. My abortion was scheduled for the following morning. I told my sister and a friend, but no one else.

We stayed at Greg's mother's house for the night and the next morning, he drove me to the clinic. I don't know what he did or where he went. I never asked and he never said. He was there waiting for me when it was over.

My recollection of that day is blurred. Most of the details have, fortunately for me, been blocked out of my mind. But the sound of that doctor's machine is forever impeded in my mind. And the room, it was so cold. They told me it wouldn't be painful and would be over quickly. They lied. It was extremely painful and I lie there for what seemed like an eternity. I remember the nurse holding my hand as the abortionist sucked my insides out. At least that's how I remember it. Almost immediately, I felt such a sense of loneliness, even though I was surrounded by several people.

Afterwards, Greg was waiting for me. We left, without ever saying a word. In the car, he still wouldn't talk or look at me. We didn't want to go back to his mother's house so we decided to stay at his grandmother's house for the night. He was to take me back to school the next morning.

The rest of the day was somber and when night came, we laid in bed together, staring at the ceiling, still not speaking.

I wanted so badly for him to hold me. I needed his arms around me to tell me it was going to be all right. But he showed no compassion for me. He didn't care what I'd been through. He just happened to be there.

A few hours passed and Greg's grandfather came into our room. He said it wasn't right that we were in the same bed together. He said Greg needed to get out and sleep in another room. He knew we were sleeping together so I couldn't understand why all of a sudden he picked this night to get moral with us. Greg didn't argue, he just quietly got up and left the room. I was alone. I remember thinking, "What a cold, cruel world I live in." In that moment, I knew that what I'd done was very wrong. It was too late. I literally felt my heart harden that night and it would take years for it to soften again.

Greg took me back to school the next day and we both knew our relationship was over. We didn't need to verbalize it. Within twenty-four hours of my abortion, I became sick. I had a very high fever and was in bed for days. My migraines continued to worsen and I was missing too many classes. I began having strange feelings and nightmares. My greatest fear was that I was going to die. I was totally paranoid about everything and everyone. I thought God was going to reach down and kill me at any moment.

Within a month of my abortion, I quit college. I had had an abortion to save my relationship with my father and further my education and now I had lost everything.

I came back home and got a job as a waitress. Mom didn't know why, but she didn't ask questions. She continued to support me. My relationship with my father continued to be strained. I began having sex with multiple partners and started drinking heavily. My lifestyle continued and within months, I went from bad to worse.

A year after my abortion, a friend and I decided to move to the beach together. By this time, I was out of control. The last partner that I had found out he had hepatitis. Anyone who had had sex with him had to be tested right away. Thank God, I was negative.

But this event shook me hard. I looked at myself in the mirror and said, "What are you doing?" It was a real wake-up call for me. I knew that if I didn't change my way of living, I would be dead.

I decided to go back home and start over again. I started looking up old friends and one of them was a guy that I knew from high school. I knew if my life was going to change for the better, I needed to hang around better people. We hooked up and started dating right away. He wasn't the type of guy I was used to and I liked that. He was "normal" and he was a good guy. I thought that if I stayed with him, he could save me from myself.

My migraines continued, as did many other ailments. Panic attacks, depression, fear and sexual problems became commonplace in my life. Thoughts of suicide plagued my mind constantly. I would envision myself driving off a cliff and ending it all. My husband just thought my problems were part of the package. He didn't ask or question why I was the way I was. He learned to live and accept me and I was doing the same.

Things got so bad that I sought out psychiatric help. The counselor never asked me if I'd had an abortion before. He didn't feel the need to ask, I suppose. He just assumed I was having "female" problems. His cure was an anti-depressant. It's not his fault, I suppose. I was as ignorant as he was in getting to the root of my problem.

Fifteen years later, married and with two children, I told him about my abortion. I never associated the problems I was having with my abortion because I had buried it so deep. I never gave myself permission to think or talk about it to anyone.

I didn't understand what was wrong with me. I had this great husband who adored me, two wonderful children. Why wasn't I happy? Why couldn't I be intimate with my husband? Am I crazy? No one could seem to help me. I knew if I was going to get the help I needed, I'd better start with me. I made the realization that my migraines had begun immediately after my decision to have an abortion and had continued ever since.

I continued to see the psychologist for three months. It didn't help. Nothing seemed to help until one day in church, I noticed a "Sanctity of Human Life" brochure in the bulletin.

I went to the pastor's wife and told her what I'd done. I said, "I had an abortion when I was 18 years old." I was shocked by the words that were coming from my mouth. I hadn't told anyone for fifteen years! I was even more shocked that I became so emotional about it. I thought I was over it! I wasn't even close. I didn't know then that my healing was just about to begin. As quick as I made my confession, I stopped. I told her "I just can't talk about this anymore."

She said, "OK."

I went away and began to cry. I couldn't stand up anymore. I fell to the floor and sobbed like a baby. I was angry that I couldn't control myself. I thought, "Why is this bothering me?" "I thought I was over it." I told my husband that I needed help. He was so supportive and loving and told me we would do whatever we had to do to get it for me.

I called the Crisis Center right away and explained to them about my abortion and what emotions I was now experiencing. I told them, "You probably have never had anyone like me call you before, but I need to know where I can get help." The woman on the other end of the line told me, "We have many." I really thought I was the only one!!

I mean, women talk about everything together, but you never hear someone in the bathroom saying, "Oh, by the way, did I ever tell you I had an abortion before?"

The counselor at the center asked me if I would like to sign up for a Post-Abortion Recover Class. I quickly said yes. I had to do something. During the classes, I continued to rationalize why I'd had an abortion. I told the women that I had no choice.

In one of the classes, we were handed a fetal development chart. It showed the development of a baby and the different stages they would be at. I went down the page to my baby's age. Twelve weeks. I couldn't believe what I was reading. My baby had ears and eye buds and a heartbeat! My baby wasn't a blob of tissue! They lied to me! I started screaming, "I killed my baby! I killed my baby!" I was inconsolable. I had convinced myself that my baby wasn't a living human being because it was easier for me to live with. I was in total denial. My baby was alive! I had taken the life of my own child. What kind of a woman takes the life of her own flesh and blood! I thought I was a monster.

This day would prove to be one of the best things that ever happened to me. This study saved my life. I continued to work hard and press through. As painful as it was, I knew I had to face what I'd done and then accept God's forgiveness. I was doing well in the study until the chapter called "Letting Go."

In this chapter, you had to let go of your child and hand your child over to God. You have to release them into His hands. I couldn't do it.

Because of my religious beliefs at the time, I wasn't sure if my baby was even in Heaven with God. I couldn't get past this in my head. My counselor suggested that we stop the bible study until I could find the answers I was looking for.

Six months had gone by and I still hadn't resolved the question of where my baby was. I cried out to God and begged Him to tell me. "Where is my baby? Is my baby with You? Please answer me God, I've got to know where my baby is!"

My daughter was singing with a Children's Choir at the time and they had made a tape. I listened to it occasionally when I was in my car. On this particular day, I immediately popped the tape in as I started my car and I couldn't believe my ears. In the most beautiful and angelic of voices, children were singing. They were saying, "If anyone asks you where I'm going, tell them I'm going to Heaven with my Father."

In that precious moment, I knew God was answering me through these wonderful children. It was the most beautiful thing I'd ever heard in my life. I didn't deserve an answer, yet He gave me one. He knew all the agony I was in and He loved me so much that He wanted to ease my pain. God couldn't have spoken more audibly to me than He did through that wonderful tape! It was a moment I shall never forget. One I still can't tell about without getting emotional. I had my answer!

I called my counselor and told her that I knew where my baby was. I knew that my child was in Heaven with God. She told me it was time. We needed to finish the last chapter of our study. And that's exactly what we did. The bible study was one of the best things that ever happened to me. My prayer is that any woman who has experience the trauma that abortion brings will find the peace and joy that I know share in my heart. I have never been the same since that bible study.

Do I ever cry over my baby? Sure I do. It is a regret I will live with for the rest of my life. But I have vowed to help others not to make the same mistakes that I, and so many millions of other women, have made. I want the truth to be known about abortion.

I am now a Post-Abortion Recovery Counselor. It is one of the most rewarding things I've done in my life. My panic attacks have subsided, my guilt is gone. You can have healing from abortion. But I believe with all of my heart that drugs won't do it. Only God can. I tried everything else and then I tried Him. He was the only One who truly helped me.

Tammy

In late 1981, I was a young, immature eighteen-year-old girl. I was working at McDonald's and this is where I met my new boyfriend. I became pregnant soon after our relationship began and my boyfriend insisted that I have an abortion. I refused and eight months later gave birth to a healthy, baby boy.

We began living together, but broke up after about three months. We continued to see each other periodically and within a few months, I was pregnant again. When I told him, he became very upset with me. He said, "How could you even want to have another one? You just had one!" He made it very clear that he didn't want the baby and that he wanted nothing to do with this pregnancy.

Two weeks later, I decided to take matters into my own hands. I made an appointment at an abortion clinic and kept it. I never told anyone. I drove myself there and again home. I literally don't remember anything about the "procedure." The one thing that I haven't forgotten was the heavy bleeding I experienced afterwards.

The clinic had given me material about abortion and I hid it in my apartment so no one would ever find it. I don't know why I just didn't throw it away.

My boyfriend never asked me about the pregnancy again. I assume he just imagined that his problem had "disappeared." We continued to see each other and had an on again, off again relationship. He was very involved in our son's life so it was necessary that we were around each other often.

I was continuing a sexual relationship with my son's father and a year later, I found myself pregnant again. This time, I told no one, not even him. What would be the use? I already knew from the past what his reaction would be. So I never told him or anyone else.

One day, my boyfriend came by to see me at work. He said, "You look like you're gaining weight." Even though I had made up my mind to abort, I continued putting the "procedure" off. I was now fourteen weeks pregnant and starting to show. I knew I had to do something soon or it would be too late. The longer I waited, I thought, the bigger chance that this "blob of tissue" would form into a "real" baby.

After he came by to see me, I panicked and realized I couldn't postpone it any longer. What was I waiting for anyway? Did I really believe anything was going to change? Was I waiting for the courage to tell him and hoping he'd change my mind?

I had created a fantasy in my head that if I told him, his response would be, "Oh, baby, everything's going to be OK. We can get married and have our baby. I love you." That was never going to happen so I called the clinic the next day and made the appointment.

When I reached the clinic, the nurse asked, "Why'd you wait so long?" I didn't have an answer. After this second abortion, I broke off the relationship. It was over.

I knew I had to get my life together. If I was ever going to have a better life for my son and me, I had better start making better decisions. I enrolled in nursing school and was doing well. Finally, I had found something I could be good at. Life was going well for me and for the first time, in a long time, my future looked promising.

I began dating a guy that I met at college and three months later, I was late. I had been down this road before, but this time I felt different. I didn't even think about the past abortions, nor did I ever want to. I just blocked them out of my mind. To this day, I don't remember anything about them.

My then boyfriend was very supportive. He said, "We can do this." I really wanted to keep this baby. At first, we had every intention of seeing this pregnancy to the end. But a few weeks later, he called me and said, "I can't go through with this. I think you should have an abortion."

He continued to persuade me that this was the most sensible solution to the challenge we were now faced with. Everything he was saying made sense so I gave in. I had already been down this road before. I was completely numb to my past abortions so I figured this time wouldn't be any different. All these years, I had blocked the previous abortions out of my mind. I thought this time wouldn't be any different. I was dead wrong.

We drove to the clinic and my boyfriend was extremely uncomfortable. He kept saying, "What if somebody sees us?"

When my name was called, I followed the nurse into the "procedure" room. They told me to lie down on the table and then immediately stuck something in my arm. I don't know what it was, but right away I became drowsy. It freaked me out and I started screaming. I tried to get off the table, but I couldn't get back up. I said, "No! I don't want to do this! No!"

The doctor came in and told the nurse, "Shut her up! She's going to scare the other girls!" It was then that the nurse placed her hand over my mouth and another held me down. The doctor came over and looked down at me and said, "What are you screaming about? This is what you wanted!" Tears streamed down my face.

With my eyes, I pleaded with them to stop. They didn't. After the doctor was finished, he slapped my thigh and said, "You can go now, you're done." The nurse had to help me walk to the recovery room, where I immediately got dressed and ran to the waiting area where my boyfriend was waiting for me.

He didn't speak until we got in the car. He said, "I heard someone screaming and thought it was you. I almost came back there."

I said, "It was me! Why didn't you come?" He didn't say another word the rest of the way home. I was still in shock. I felt so violated and betrayed. This was the worst experience I have ever had in my life.

Why didn't they stop? What were they worried about? Their money! They could have had their money! I wanted my baby! For the first time since my first abortion, it hit me on that table. I was about to kill my own flesh and blood! My own precious child. And this wasn't the first time either!

From that day on, I was never the same. I went home and climbed into bed. I was inconsolable and wanted to be alone. My boyfriend was experiencing his own guilt as he realized that the cries for help were mine and he did nothing. I had to live with what I'd done and so did he now.

I not only couldn't stop thinking about this last abortion, but now the previous abortions were hitting me hard. I experienced panic attacks on a daily basis and lost all interest in sex. I was too paranoid of ever getting pregnant again. Birth control wasn't an option because I was using birth control each time I got pregnant!

I stayed with my boyfriend for the next seven years. I never got pregnant again. It's difficult to get pregnant when you refuse to have sex. On numerous occasions I would ask him, "Do you feel bad about what happened? Do you think about what we did?" His answer was always the same, "I don't want to talk about it." And so, we never did.

I began having dreams about Jesus and me. I had gone to church as a child, but never really thought much about God. In my dreams Jesus was writing with his finger in a pile of ashes. I couldn't tell what He was writing, but I could see his finger moving as if He was trying to tell me something.

The next Sunday, I attended a church service. The pastor preached a sermon and towards the end said, "Jesus is going to give someone here beauty for ashes." I remembered my dream, but couldn't understand what I could have done so bad that He would be saying this to me? I was still trying to deny that my abortions were wrong. This was the way I dealt with it. There was no way I could think of myself as a mother who would murder her own children. I hadn't realized that my emotional, physical and sexual problems all stemmed from my abortions. I kept burying those memories as far down as possible.

Then the pastor said it again, "Jesus is going to give you beauty for ashes. It doesn't matter what you've done, maybe someone here has even had an abortion." When I heard the word, "abortion," I cringed. He was talking about me! I didn't wait for him to ask, I ran to the altar. I begged God for forgiveness and I wept until I couldn't cry anymore. In that moment, I knew that I was carrying the guilt and shame of my abortions everywhere I went. And in an instant, I felt forgiven. Now it was time for me to learn to accept that forgiveness and to forgive myself.

I found a Crisis Pregnancy Center in my town right away and called. I wanted to volunteer as a counselor so I could help other women. During the first training session, the trainer asked if anyone had ever had an abortion before. She said if you had and felt comfortable, stand up. A few women stood, but I wasn't one of them.

I wasn't ready to reveal my secret just yet. I didn't know if I ever would be. I still hadn't been able to say out loud, even to myself, "I had an abortion." There was no way I saw myself at this point telling it to someone else, especially a stranger.

A few days after the training class, the instructor called me. She said, "Tammy, there's going to be an abortion recovery weekend coming up for women who've had abortions. I really think you should consider going." I said, "Why did you call me?" She replied, "Because I saw you stand up the other night." I was stunned. I hadn't stood up. I made sure of it.

Was there an angel pointing at me saying, "Over here, this one needs some major help!" I didn't know. But one thing I was sure of was that I hadn't stood up. Yet, here she was calling me. I told her again, "I never stood up, but you're right. I did have an abortion. I don't know how you knew that, but it's true. Yes, I would like to go." She signed me up.

At the time, I was totally prepared to go. I was even kind of excited. But as the time drew closer for the weekend to begin, I started chickening out. I was too afraid. How could it help me anyway? I made up my mind not to go. I would just make up an excuse and apologize. Yes, that should work.

One of the counselors for the weekend called me. She said she was excited about my participation in the program. She reassured me how wonderful it was going to be for me. I told her that I was having second thoughts. She wouldn't take no for an answer. She insisted that I must be there. She just knew that the Lord had something special for me.

She was right. Upon her urging, I agreed to go. I have never regretted that decision. Those were the best three-and-a-half days of my life. The Lord cleansed me and made me whole again.

When I returned home from the weekend, my husband commented that I even looked different. I told him that that was only the beginning. I felt different too. My heart had finally been healed from the torments of my past.

I thank the Lord for the abortion recovery retreats. I am so thankful that I am not living in the hell that I was growing used to.

I will forever regret the decisions that I made to abort my children. But I am grateful to a God who forgives, heals and sets you free.

Pat

I could tell you about the other two abortions that I've had, but to be quite honest with you, I don't remember anything about them. I was too high on drugs to even remember who took me or what exactly happened. I can tell you one thing I know for sure. I was pregnant twice and then within a few moments, I wasn't anymore. I can also tell you with complete conviction that my decision to abort cost me years of grief that will continue for the rest of my life. Although, I have found true healing through Jesus Christ's love, I still live with the pain of knowing what I've done. Nothing can ever change the fact that I aborted not only two, but three children.

The story that I want to tell you about is my third abortion. I remember this one as if it were yesterday.

My boyfriend and I were about to be married when we found out that we were pregnant. Finally, I was beginning to get my life together. I had gotten off drugs and was in cosmetology school. For the first time in my life, I felt my life might count for something and that I could actually make something of myself.

We didn't want to start our marriage off with a child so we mutually agreed that abortion would be a quick, easy solution. When we arrived at the clinic, there were picketers in the front of the building. They were screaming at all of the women and waving signs in their faces. My boyfriend decided to take me around the back of the building. He dropped me off and then he left. He would be back in a few hours to pick me up.

When I entered the clinic, I was taken into the "counseling" room with several other women. It was here that the "counselor" would explain our upcoming procedure. She had with her what I would call a flip chart. She began inquiring as to how far along each of us were. One girl was six weeks, one was eight, one was ten and then I was twelve.

Each time we answered her question, she would flip to the size of the "thing" we were carrying in our bodies. All of the pictures looked the same. The pictures resembled something that didn't look human. It looked more like an alien. A group of cells, she called "it." The only differences in the pictures were the sizes.

I was the farthest along so my picture was the largest. Still not resembling anything close to a human baby, I was relieved. It was much easier to abort something that wasn't "real" yet.

We were then lead into separate rooms where the "procedure" would take place. I love how they use the words, "not a human being yet" and "procedure." They are very careful about the words they say. I feel sure they're trained in the phrases that they use.

The doctor entered the room and got ready. He never made eye contact with me and he never spoke or acknowledged me. There were two nurses with me. One stood by my head and the other assisted the doctor.

Due to the stage of my pregnancy, they would be using the suctioning method to perform my abortion. As the doctor turned the machine on, the noise was terribly loud. It was so loud that had I been able to speak, no one would have heard me anyway.

It didn't take him long and then it was over. He handed one of the nurses the machine and she walked over to the sink to empty the contents. I know now that she was counting body parts to make sure they'd gotten everything. The next thing that struck me to the core was what she said. Without looking away from the sink, she announced, "Oh, you had a girl."

I was shocked. How could she tell? From the picture I'd seen earlier, I was carrying a blob of tissue. It hadn't even looked human, let alone resembled anything close to a girl or boy. How could she tell? I desperately wanted an answer, but I never asked.

Still in a total state of shock, I was lifted from the table and taken into the recovery room. The cots were full of young girls and women. Some were crying and some were chatting with nurses. No one consoled each other. Everyone wanted to be left alone. I was offered cookies and milk, but I declined. All I knew was that I wanted out of there as quickly as possible. I called my boyfriend and asked him to hurry.

When I got in the car, I continued to cry. I began begging a God that I didn't serve to forgive me. Something inside of me longed for His forgiveness. For the first time, I knew that I had just taken the life of another person. A life that was given to me as a gift and now a part of me was gone. Just like that, my baby girl was gone.

My boyfriend drove me to work. I needed to stay busy and thought working would be the best way to do that. Within an hour, I had to leave. I didn't feel well and was started running a high fever. I went home and stayed in bed for the rest of the day. I was so frightened. I became paranoid and imagined how God would kill me for what I'd done. I kept waiting for Him to strike me down. I was sure He was going to take my three-year-old son from me. I was depressed the rest of the week. Soon, it would be my wedding day. This should be the most wonderful time of my life, but it was the grimmest.

My boyfriend and I went through with our wedding a week later. No one knew what we had done just a few days before. I told my husband that I didn't feel we would ever be given a chance to have another child, but within a few years, I was pregnant again. I was so happy and determined to take care of myself. I had to do everything in my power to have a healthy baby. I tried to be a better person so that God wouldn't punish me or take this baby from me.

Throughout my pregnancy, I was terrified that something would go wrong. I was having nightmares that my baby would be deformed or born dead. I couldn't believe that there was a God who would bless with me with a healthy, normal baby. I had killed three of my own children. How could He allow me a chance to be a mother again?

I didn't enjoy my pregnancy, as I would have liked to. I was too afraid of getting attached to this child growing inside of me. I was so sure God was going to take this baby at any moment.

Months later, I gave birth to a healthy and beautiful baby girl. A girl! I couldn't believe it! I had secretly prayed for a girl. She was perfect and I cherished her.

I continued to live in fear of losing her and it was destroying me. I told my husband I wanted to go to church. I had to do "good things" so God wouldn't hate me and take one of my children. I couldn't bear the thought of losing one of them for what I had done. It wasn't their sin—it was mine.

My husband and I began attending church and it was at one of the services that I asked Christ into my life. I practically ran to the altar and begged Him for forgiveness for taking the lives of my children. I repented and He forgave me of everything I'd ever done. I cried as I'd never cried before. I felt so free for the first time in so many years.

I experienced a sense of peace that I'd never had in my life. I knew that if a God such as this could forgive me and set me free, I would serve Him for the rest of my life.

I knew the day would come when I would have to confess to my children what had happened to their siblings. My daughter had always wanted a sister and I knew that I had aborted at least one girl. I prayed for God to open the door when the time would be right to tell her.

When my daughter was fourteen years old, she was given a class assignment on writing. She had to pick and write about someone she admired. She chose me. This was the door I was looking for and I walked through it. I knew that it was time to tell her the ugly truth about my past. I knew it was risky, but somehow I knew everything was going to be OK.

I shared with her all that I'd done. I waited for her response. What I'd feared most never happened. She didn't hate me. Just as Christ still loved and accepted me, my daughter did the same.

Within a few months, I was sharing my testimony at my church. I'm sure they were shocked, but it was something I had to do. Some women take their "secret" to their graves. I chose to bring mine out. The truth truly does "set you free."

If one child is saved from abortion because of my story, then it's worth the risk I take in telling it.

I am now a Director of a Crisis Pregnancy Center in my town, where I share my story with many who are abortion minded. Women need to be told the whole truth about what abortion is about. It is the killing of an innocent child. It isn't the easy solution we're told. So many women are being lied to regarding abortion. Yes, there is forgiveness and healing in Jesus Christ. I am a living testimony to that. I know I'm forgiven and it helps me to live with my abortion, but I will never forget.

It's time that abortion minded women were told the truth about how devastating this choice can be on your life. I hope and pray that they will make the right one. Women were created to create life and nurture it. It goes against our nature to kill our own children and when the post-abortive woman realizes what she's done, it can have catastrophic consequences.

I have two wonderful children and I treasure my relationship with them. I wish to God I had five.

Sabrina

My name is Sabrina. I am 3 ½ years post-abortive. I want to tell you that God is a loving and forgiving God and the great Healer! He has forgiven and set me free from the bondage of my sin and the guilt and shame I have felt ever since my abortion.

I found out I was pregnant in April of 1999. I couldn't believe the home pregnancy test was reading positive. I screamed out loud! The baby's father was downstairs waiting for the results and secretly hoping it was a negative one. He knew the test was positive as soon as he heard me scream. I immediately went downstairs and confirmed his suspicions. I was indeed pregnant.

In that instant, he told me I could not keep this baby. He said that I must have an abortion! Although, at that time, I was not walking with the Lord, I knew that abortion was wrong. Several years earlier, I had given my life to Jesus, but by this time, I had walked away from God. I didn't want to have an abortion. I told the baby's father this, but he didn't care what I wanted. He gave me what he called options, but they all came back to one thing, having an abortion.

He and I already had one child together, a beautiful seven-month-old boy. He had nothing to do with our son, as it was, so I don't know why I thought he would be demanding anything less than an abortion. He made it very clear that he wouldn't have anything to do with this child either. I broke down and cried.

I love my son. I had so badly wanted him to know his dad. I rationalized that maybe if I did what the father wanted, he would become the father that my son deserved. I had never met my own biological father and would have done anything for my son to know his own father.

I was so confused! I began to believe the lies he was telling me. He told me I couldn't make it on my own as a single mom with two children. I didn't have a college education and I felt like he was right. Without an education, how could I possibly take care of two children without help from their father? I convinced myself that he was right. I knew I couldn't financially afford a second child. I also knew this child would also be fatherless and I was sure that I couldn't give this child a good life. The baby's father had won.

He told me that we needed to call right away and make an appointment for the abortion. He said the quicker, the better. Since, according to him, this "blob of tissue" wasn't a baby yet, it would make it easier on both of us. I agreed. The earlier, the better.

I made the phone call to the clinic. I couldn't believe I was actually going through with it. I wanted to say, "No, thanks, I've changed my mind." But I didn't. Everything was happening so fast. I didn't allow myself time for anything to sink in. Before I knew it, I was off the phone with an appointment made right away.

I was so upset with myself. My baby's father was relieved. He said he would get the money together right away. The clinic said they would only accept cash.

Even though I had stopped going to church, I got on the phone and started calling people with whom I used to attend church. I know now that I was hoping someone would talk me out of what I was about to do. I desperately wanted someone to stop me. Only one person from church said they would help me. That was it. One. She was a good friend and said I could come to her house. She didn't want me home when my baby's father came back with the cash. She offered to let me stay with her. I never went.

I told my mother and even my grandparents that I was pregnant. I was hoping they would make me keep this baby and talk sense in to me! But they didn't. The ultimate decision, though, was mine.

The night before the abortion, the baby's father came back to my house. He stayed the night to make sure I wouldn't change my mind. He slept downstairs on my couch and I slept upstairs. I was so angry, I couldn't even look at him.

The next morning, my mother agreed to watch our son so we could go to the clinic. I told my mother where I was going. I wanted her to stop me. She herself was a single mom with two children. I needed to hear her say that she loved me. I needed her encouragement. I needed her to tell me that I could make it–that she would help me. She didn't. She just frowned and watched me leave.

We drove to the clinic in silence. When I got out of the car, there were abortion protestors picketing, holding up signs and yelling at me that I was a murderer! I quickly made my way into the clinic. The clinic workers told me not to worry about the protestors. They said that they do that all the time.

It was crowded inside. At least twenty people were sitting there waiting, along with me, to kill their babies. I remember a twelve-year-old girl crying to her mother that she didn't want to kill her baby. The girl's mother was arguing with her, telling her that she had no choice. She was only twelve! I could feel that girl's pain! I, too, felt forced into having an abortion. I was convinced I had no other choice.

There was a counselor there who asked me if I was certain that I wanted to go through with the abortion. Everything in me wanted to scream "NO!" But, instead, I handed her the $300 cash. I kept repeating over and over to myself, "I'm only four weeks pregnant, it's still just tissue."

It was the worst decision I've ever made. I lay there in a cold room with my feet in stirrups. They vacuumed the baby out of me. I was told not to look, but I did. I saw what looked like blood being flushed out of me. All I could do was imagine that I was actually witnessing my own baby's body parts being sucked out of me. I wanted to throw up. I told myself, "I have to be strong, it's not a baby. Remember, it's no big deal, it's only a yolk sack."

The doctor kept telling me it was ok. He said it was only tissue. He lied to me! There was a nurse in the room holding my hand. She was eight months pregnant. I acted very nonchalant and congratulated her. How different our circumstances were. I wondered how she could keep her conscience clear, holding my hand knowing what I was doing when she was pregnant. The radio was on. The song playing was called "What's it like" by a group known as Everlast. Midway during the song, they were singing about a girl having an abortion. This song was playing at the exact moment my abortion was being performed.

Afterwards, I was taken to the recovery room. It was very cold. I was trying to forget about what I'd just done. I was in a lot of pain, cramping severely and bleeding. Everyone at the clinic was very nice to me. They wanted to reassure me that I had made the right decision. They lied to me too.

As soon as we left the clinic, I opened my purse and pulled out a small amount of marijuana. I brought it on purpose, I didn't want to feel anything. I smoked it and passed it to my baby's father. We just tried to act nothing had happened. He dropped me off at my house and I lay on the couch for the rest of the night. I was still in pain and bleeding heavily.

For the next three and a half years, I lived my life in deep depression. I led a self-destructive lifestyle, yet I wasn't sure why I was so unhappy. I did everything and anything to keep from feeling the hurt and pain from my abortion. Daily, I pretended it never happened.

Recently, I rededicated my life to Jesus Christ. I constantly asked God to forgive me for the sin of my abortion, yet I never felt forgiven. How could He forgive me for such a thing? I carried guilt and shame everywhere I went. Condemning myself became a habit. I told myself that I was a horrible person and didn't deserve to live. My baby's birthday was always on my mind, as well as thoughts of whether it was a boy or girl and what he or she would have looked like. I cried all the time.

I found out about an abortion healing class and during that class, I learned that I had been lied to. My baby wasn't a blob of tissue! My baby was a life, a gift from God! My baby was alive from the day of conception. Even at four weeks pregnant, my baby had a heartbeat and my baby's arms, legs and eyes were beginning to form. My baby even had a nervous system! The realization that I came to was that I had committed murder, I actually killed my own baby!

I was so angry with everyone associated with my abortion. Why didn't they stop me? I was even angry with God. After acknowledging those I was angry with, I was finally able to start forgiving and I have been able to forgive them all. I had to take responsibility for the fact that I had taken the life of my unborn child. The ultimate responsibility was mine.

After many hours of counseling and soul searching, I was able to accept God's forgiveness. I've learned that it's not a feeling, not something I can earn. Through God's love, mercy and grace, He forgave me. Forgiving myself took a lot longer.

I asked the Lord to reveal the sex of my baby to me. She was a girl. I named her, Jordan Elizabeth and I know she's in Heaven. I believe that on the day I get there, she will meet me at the pearly gates with Jesus by her side.

My grandparents have told me that they will look for Jordan when they get to Heaven. I deeply regret my decision to abort Jordan. I know that I am greatly loved by God and that he not only forgave me, He also healed my wounds and took away the bitterness that was eating me alive. Through prayer, God's Word and counseling, I have been able to receive healing. Life is a gift from God and for the rest of mine I plan to treasure it!

This next story comes with a warning. If you are faint at heart, or weak in the stomach, you may want to skip this one. This particular woman, Ingrid, uses graphic details of the abortion she witnessed. Parental discretion is highly advised.

Abortion is not a pretty subject, as this actual story will reveal. I contemplated editing the details of the actual abortion, but decided against it. This book is not going to sugar coat what really happens during an abortion. But, please be advised, that this is the only story in the book that comes with such a warning. Please read at your own risk.

Ingrid

It took many thoughtful hours to decide if I wanted to be a part of this book. I knew that reliving the past can sometimes be excruciatingly painful. Especially a past such as the one I am about to share with you. But after hours of careful consideration and prayer, I came to the conclusion that my story had to be told. I feel sharing what happened to me could literally change the course of someone else's life. This was not an easy project by any means. As a matter of fact, I believe it has been the hardest thing I've ever done in my life. It helps that each time I tell my story, I experience a little bit more freedom from the guilt and shame of my past.

In 1995, I was a very happy nineteen-year-old college student. I was in school on a full basketball scholarship, dating a great guy and having the time of my life. My boyfriend was from a very prominent and wealthy family in Venezuela. One evening, his sister called and wanted to come for a visit. She said she was desperate to learn English and eager to visit the United States. She was also nineteen and I was excited about the idea of meeting and getting to know her.

Within two days of our first meeting, she informed me that she was six months pregnant. You couldn't tell by the looks of her. She was painfully thin. She desperately wanted an abortion. She insisted that she must have one. Because of her family situation in Venezuela, it was impossible for her to receive an abortion there without them finding out. She asked me if I would help her. Her English was poor and she would need an interpreter. I am fluent in Spanish and I didn't see why not. I said yes.

I was raised in a Christian family and always active in the church and community. Somehow, I blocked everything I'd ever been taught about abortion out of mind. She was my new friend and she needed my help. In my mind, I was only doing a favor for a friend. To me, it couldn't be any more plain or simple than that. I'd always considered myself to be a good person. I took pride in being a good friend to anyone who needed one. Besides, I thought, "It's not my body, it's not my child." I looked at the situation with a different set of eyes than I normally would, completely disregarding my own personal opinion about the matter. I felt that it wasn't my duty to play God or change her mind. My point of view on the subject wasn't the issue, so I thought. Maybe this was my way of dealing with it.

We made some phone calls and found out about an abortion clinic in Melbourne, Florida. When we arrived, there were pro-life advocates surrounding the building. They were holding up signs, expressing their beliefs and harassing any of the ladies that would dare enter the clinic. There were news cameras everywhere. My friend and I couldn't take a chance of being recognized so we decided to wear disguises. We had to make sure neither of our families ever found out what we were about to do. For them to see us on the nightly news was too much to even think about! That could have been devastating to our futures.

Because she was so far along in the pregnancy, they informed us that they wouldn't be able to perform the abortion. We were referred to another clinic in Daytona Beach. The doctor there was the only one they knew of that could or would perform such a late term abortion.

We got back in our car and drove to Daytona. When we arrived at the clinic, we were told the cost was significantly higher than usual. Remember, she was six months along in her pregnancy. We didn't have the $3,500.00 they wanted to perform the abortion, so we had no choice but to leave. We drove home making plans how to get the money.

We asked for help from everyone we could. We never told anyone why we needed the money, only that it was an emergency. Somehow we gathered up the $3,500.00 we would need.

With our funds now in place, we called the clinic and made an appointment. They were more than happy to oblige us. During our first visit, they showed us a video explaining the "procedure" and each of the tools that would be used to perform it. They never once referred to it as an abortion.

According to this video, it didn't look like a big deal. There wasn't much to it. She was just "terminating a pregnancy."

We met the doctor and he explained everything. It sounded simple enough. He would begin her first set of "treatments" on this day. He explained to us what he would be doing. He said he would have to insert a laminarias dilapan (an applicator inserted into her vagina to dilate the cervix) to open up her cervix. This would have to be done repeatedly over the next couple of weeks before the actual abortion would take place. I stayed with my friend as he performed the dilation. She seemed a little uncomfortable, but not in a lot of pain.

We were then told to return within three days to have the dilation procedure repeated. Each time we visited, we scheduled our next appointment up until the final and actual day of the abortion. During each of our two-and-a-half hour trips to and from the doctor's office, neither of us said a word.

The final day arrived. This last trip would prove to be the longest. It was the day of the abortion. I think I was more frightened than she was. Should I say something? Was this my time to talk her out of it? Was I supposed to try and stop her from going through with it? It wasn't too late at this point, but she did seem determined. Her mind was made up. It was none of my business! So, I didn't bother trying. When we arrived, we were taken into a cold room where the abortion would take place. It was clean and sterile, much like a hospital operating room.

My friend was given anesthesia and she asked me if I could hold her hand during the procedure. I told her I would. The anesthesia would only numb her slightly and she would be awake throughout the entire process.

Before they began the actual abortion, the nurse did a sonogram to determine the location of the baby. She showed us the screen and made the comment, "Your baby boy is so tiny." She said it so matter-of-factly that it took me by surprise. I wasn't surprised by what she'd said, considering my friend practically starved herself so she wouldn't gain any weight. You could barely tell she was pregnant at all. I was only surprised because it was the first time she referred to him as a baby. But there he was, a baby boy. He was moving around, minding his own business. He had no idea what was about to hit him. There it was, proof that another human being was growing and living inside of her body. That should have been enough for us to run out of that room, but we didn't. We stayed until the end.

The doctor came in and began his work. He opened up her cervix with a succession of dilation. He talked to my friend through the entire process. I interpreted every word. He never asked if she wanted to change her mind. My friend never spoke. She didn't ask any questions, she just lay there. He never gave me permission to leave if I'd wanted to. He explained in detail everything he was doing or about to do. She ignored him. She kept looking around the room, never focusing on what he was saying or what he was doing. She seemed not to care. It was obvious that she just wanted him to hurry up and finish.

What you're about to read should come with a warning, so here it is. The details of my friend's abortion are extremely graphic, but abortion is not like having a pap smear, it's very ugly. What I'm about to share with you will sound unbelievable, but it's true. I should know because I was there.

Towards the end of the abortion, the doctor used a pliers-like instrument to literally chop up the baby. This was because he said the baby's bones and skull were calcified. With a twisting motion, the doctor seized a part of the body and tore it from the baby's body. He repeated this again and again in order to snap the spine and skull so that he could remove them. The little guy never had a chance. I held my breath as I waited for him to scream. He never did.

The cannula was attached to the electrical pump that would extract the contents of the uterus, including the baby. The pump was clear and I watched horrified as each body part was sucked into the vacuum like instrument and then finally into the pump. A curette (a spoon-like instrument) was used to scrape the walls of the uterus and to remove any remaining tissue.

I wasn't holding her hand anymore. Instead, I was holding myself up. I was in a total state of shock at what was happening. I couldn't move. I couldn't believe what I just witnessed. For the first time since this ordeal had begun, I wanted to run as fast as I could from this God forsaken place. I wanted no part of it. I knew within minutes that we had all just taken part in murdering an innocent little baby boy. I wanted to scream, but no words would form in my mouth. I wanted out of there! How had I let myself get involved in this massacre! Was this some kind of a nightmare! Unfortunately for me, it wasn't. I was wide-awake caught up in a living hell!

The murder took only twenty minutes, but to me it was like an eternity. When it was over, we left in silence. She didn't want to stay in recovery. We agreed that we just wanted to leave right away. Two days later, my "friend" was back on her feet. She acted as if nothing had ever happened. We never spoke of this again. Our friendship ended as quickly as it had begun. For years, I never spoke of this incident to anyone. I tried not to think about it. That was not about to happen, my nightmares were only just beginning.

When I returned to school, I couldn't keep my mind on anything, except the abortion. Each time I closed my eyes, I could see him. He was just a tiny, innocent baby, alive one minute and dead the next. I couldn't get the images out of my mind. I opened up my Bible to Job 10:8-12. When I read the passages, I was terrified.

I was convinced that I just needed time. In time, I was sure that I would be over this whole thing. I would just forget about it within days, maybe weeks. I mean it wasn't like it had happened to me! I wasn't the one who killed my baby! My hands hadn't shed his innocent blood! Her hands would carry that guilt, not mine!

I thought, "OK, I would just need some time." Then I'll be back to normal. I'll be happy again. I was wrong.

Almost immediately, I began drinking and partying heavily. At the time, it was the only way I could numb the pain of what I'd done. I couldn't concentrate on my classes. Eventually, I stopped going to school altogether. Of course, my grades dropped drastically and it wasn't long before I'd lost my full scholarship. My dreams were vanishing and I couldn't do anything to stop them. I prayed day and night, even though I couldn't sense God's presence. I couldn't imagine that He would listen to me! Why would He want to help me after what I'd done?

I cried all the time. No one understood what was wrong with me because I couldn't tell. I was angry, bitter and depressed. There was no joy in my life whatsoever. I broke up with my boyfriend. I wanted no one around that would be a reminder of what had happened.

I questioned what kind of a friend would allow another friend to do such a thing? How could I have let her do it? How could I have been any part of it? I had so many questions, but I didn't have any answers. I was so afraid if others knew what I'd done, they would judge or hate me. There was no one I could talk to about it. I thought about God a lot. What must He think of me? He was right there in that room that day. I knew He witnessed the whole ugly thing. He'd watched and grieved for that precious little boy. The pain God must have felt as the doctor tore that baby to pieces, one by one.

I've loved God all my life. The thought of Him being disappointment in me was devastating. Why! Why! Why didn't the doctor or nurses tell me that I would experience such remorse! They should have warned me! They lied when they said it was a "simple procedure!" They should have stopped me from being taking a part in their butchering! They didn't. They never even tried.

For five years of my life, I was in a constant state of depression. No drug, drink or psychiatrist could numb my pain. I prayed for God to help me. Then one day, I felt drawn to church. When I entered the church service one Sunday morning that's when my healing began.

At the conclusion of the service, an invitation was given to ask Jesus Christ to come into my heart. The preacher promised that if I would ask, then Jesus would forgive me of all my sins. I couldn't believe it! Was this the answer to my questions? I didn't need a second invitation. I didn't walk, I ran to the altar and begged God for His mercy for what I'd done. I desperately needed my life to feel "normal" again.

And in literally an instant, He did as I asked. I immediately felt the weight of all that had happened leave me. I didn't deserve it, but He granted me grace and mercy, even in spite of myself.

I've never been able to talk about this with anyone without feeling tremendous sadness. This event will never be far from my mind and I will never forget that day. It will be with me until the day I die. I never want to forget the pain and agony I've experienced for that decision. It is my prayer to keep others from making the same mistake I did. No friendship was worth the price I paid for being a part of that tragedy.

I thank God daily for His grace and mercy. My healing continues each day because of God's. If it weren't for Him, I would still be living in guilt and shame, but He covers me. Maybe I'm not where I need to be yet, but I'm not where I was either. And God gets all the glory for that.

Lindsay & Joe

It was the spring of 1976. I was a senior in college and dating a wonderful guy! Since it was the 70s, the aftermath of the peace, love and sexual revolution movement, we had begun a mutually satisfying "physical expression of our love."

What had begun on the firm foundation of friendship had now blossomed into love. We shared the same values, the same likes and dislikes and we were best friends! My life and plans were "on track" and then it happened. I became pregnant!

When my period was late, I went down to the University Medical Center for a pregnancy test. As I was waiting for my test results, I was so apprehensive about the results that I sneaked a look at my chart. As I examined my file, the word leaped up from the page–Positive!

Feeling shocked and a little surreal, I moved as in slow motion back into the examine room. My thoughts and feelings, however, were swishing through my head so fast I couldn't think. How could this have happened? I was using birth control! What was I going to do? I couldn't have a baby! How could I start and finish my graduate degree? What would Joe say? What would my parents say?

I had all these plans and none of them included quitting school or moving back home with my parents and having a baby.

The doctor returned and began to give me the news when I stopped him and told him I already knew. He was silent for a moment then asked me what I wanted to do. We discussed my options and I chose abortion. At the time, it seemed like the easiest and quickest solution to my "problem." Little did I know that my problems were only beginning.

When I broke the news to Joe, he immediately offered to "do the right thing." He loved me and wanted to get married, but all I could think about was how this was going to upset all my plans. Talk about being selfish. In the end, as always, he gave in to my wishes.

We called Planned Parenthood and made the appointment for that Friday. It was surprisingly easy. On a cool, sunny day in March, we made the trip to the clinic in silence. When we arrived, we were ushered into a conference room. There, we were again silent during the short "counseling session" they administered before the "procedure." There were five or six other couples there as well. While the men remained in the waiting room, we were ushered into the next room. I was anxious for it to be over with, but not really afraid.

I really believed it wasn't anything to worry about. According to the nurse that had counseled us, it wasn't really a baby anyway. It was just a lump of tissue they were removing and it would be over quickly.

We were told to remove our clothing from the waist down and instructed to lie back on a recliner type of apparatus they had lined up side by side. I laid down next to a dark haired girl about my age that I had struck up a conversation with earlier. She seemed really nervous before and now was very scared. My future career plans were to be a counselor, so naturally I was concerned about her.

As the doctor began to move down the abortion "assembly line" of women, I began to try to allay her tears. I couldn't figure out why she was so afraid. "It's just like having a pelvic exam. It'll be over with quickly. It won't be much longer now." I whispered to her. She couldn't tell me or didn't know herself why she was so frightened. She became more and more agitated as the doctor moved closer and closer towards us. I couldn't quite figure it out. Why was she so upset? What was the big deal?

When the doctor got to her she began to cry openly. My heart went out to her. I felt sorry for her. I talked to her during the entire "procedure." She just cried harder and harder. When the doctor was finished with her, it was my turn. Then I understood.

Since there were no privacy curtains, you could talk to each other and even watch the doctor move down the line as he performed each woman's abortion. I was so busy trying to comfort the girl beside me that I wasn't prepared for what was going to happen.

To this day, I can remember the cold instrument in his hand and the noise–the loud swooshing of the vacuum device. I felt this excruciating cramp, this huge pain! Wait a minute! They told me it wouldn't hurt. They lied, it really hurt. Why would they tell me that? Why didn't they just tell me the truth so I could be prepared? Oh no, maybe something was wrong! I didn't know it yet, but something was wrong. Something was very wrong and wouldn't be right again for many years to come. I couldn't explain it exactly, but there was an empty space inside me that nothing could or would fill for a long time. I had no idea how this day would affect the next twenty-four years of my life. I truly believed my "problem" had been solved. In reality, my problems were only just beginning.

Joe and I left when it was over, but we never talked about it. We left the experience there in that clinic, along with our aborted baby. It was understood between the two of us that we were never to talk about it again. And we never did. That is, not until twenty-four years later would we speak of it.

A year and a half later, Joe and I got married. I had married my best friend and life was wonderful! By that time, I had put the abortion behind me. I had tied it up in a neat little bundle and put it away on the back shelf of my mind. I reasoned that it was over with. I couldn't take it back so I had to just get on with my life.

One night, about six months later, I had my first panic attack. I was sitting in a graduate studies class and it came over me from out of nowhere. My heart began to race. As my chest constricted in fear, I could only take short breaths. I wanted to get up and run out of the classroom, but I was convinced that my legs wouldn't hold me. I could only see within a three-foot radius and the scene was blurred around the edges.

It was very unreal. My first thought was "I must be having a heart attack." But there was no pain. My second thought was that I must be losing my mind.

It passed within a few minutes and I was amazed that no one seemed to notice. I played it off well. It was at that moment, I realized that no matter what turmoil was churning around inside of me, I was able to put on an academy award performance of normality.

Somehow, I made it to my car. It took about fifteen minutes before I felt I could drive home. I had so much adrenaline coursing through my body that I actually ached all over.

From that point on, anxiety became my constant companion. Full-blown panic attacks were thrown in from time to time just to make me appreciate plain old everyday fear.

I began to have fears of leaving my house and I was afraid to be around people. If I had to be in a social setting, I felt surreal. It was like I had stepped outside of myself. I could smile and talk with people, but it was like someone else was speaking the words coming from my mouth.

As the years went by, the panic attacks increased in frequency and severity. I had no idea where they were coming from or that they could have been caused by anything I had done or was doing. The abortion never entered my mind as the cause. I decided to seek counseling and the counselor gave me bio-feed back exercises to do. I sought help from my doctor and he said I was just a "nervous" person and gave me tranquilizers. I took prescription medication for fifteen years. That probably helped me keep from getting sick, but nothing helped alleviate my anxiety.

I came to my own conclusion that I was mentally ill and would have to live this way for the rest of my life. It was a hollow existence.

On top of my "mental illness," my love life with Joe was literally non-existent. Just the thought of ever getting pregnant again was too terrifying to me. Although our sex life before had been fairly good and normal, vaginal sex had become too painful for me to bear, so we restrained from it. I rationalized that it had to be a "physical problem."

After my abortion, I was so afraid of doctors that I never went back to a gynecologist again. I continued to see my medical doctor, a general practitioner, for my yearly exams. I would listen to my friends talk about how they disliked their visits. It was the one doctor's appointment they dreaded. Thinking about it made me so sick that I had to "zone out" on tranquilizers just to get through them. They were always very painful and left me feeling extremely violated.

During this time, we adopted a five-year-old little boy and later his eleven-year-old brother. I sat back and allowed people to think I was noble and socially conscience, while shamefully hiding my secret fear of pregnancy.

As time passed and I got worse, my husband Joe seemed to get better and better. He had started going to a church in our community and had gotten "saved." He began to take the boys with him to Sunday School and

Church every week. I played the good little wife and started going with them, more out of egotism than any real sense of dedication.

Joe, in the meantime, was growing in his walk with God. He seemed to have something I didn't have. In this loveless, sexless marriage of ours, inside, I was withering away, while he was flourishing. He began to read his bible and pray. I thought to myself, "I'm just as good a Christian as he is." Almost competitively, I began to pray to God. I asked Him to reveal what was wrong with me.

Why was I so afraid all the time? Why couldn't I get close to my husband and children? Why couldn't I feel? Why was I so controlling? Why couldn't I cry? No one else was able to answer my questions so I thought I should give God a try.

One Sunday at church, I noticed a flyer in the church bulletin from the Crisis Pregnancy Center. They were looking for counselors and were starting training classes the next month. It tugged at my conscience, but I dismissed the idea immediately.

The following Sunday, there it was again. Again, I though, "I could do this. I've had training as a counselor. I have adopted children, so I could offer an alternative to women seeking abortion." But, again, I chickened out.

When it appeared again the third Sunday, I casually asked the church secretary about it. She told me, "I usually only include the inserts for one Sunday, but felt very strongly that the Lord was leading me to continue placing it there." I was stunned!

Was it possible that God was speaking directly to me? Am I the reason it is still finding its way into the bulletin? I was afraid to call, but I was more afraid not to. That very day I called and signed up for the training classes. I was so sure I was the answer to their prayers! Yet, they would soon become the answer to mine! I just didn't know it yet!

As I began attending the training classes, I noticed the other women in the group would become emotional anytime pictures or videos were shown about abortion. Yet I sat there each time emotionless, feeling nothing. I started to question what kind of person I was. How could I be so cold and unfeeling? What was wrong with me?

The director of the center taught the training classes. I had told her about my abortion when I signed up and she hadn't "blinked an eye." She was also very careful to keep my admission form confidential from the other members of the group. I felt my "secret" was safe and began confiding in her many of the problems I had been having for so long.

I told her about the panic attacks, the sexual dysfunction and the fear of *what*? She asked me if I was aware that all of these things were very common in post-abortive women. I was skeptical. I had packed that away for so long. I hadn't even thought about it since the day I had it done. I told her that there was no way the two were related. She didn't argue with me. She just left it alone at that.

The problem was that I couldn't leave it alone. It began to nag at me. Could it be that simple? There was only one way to answer that question. As I began to mentally move down my long list of problems I asked myself, "When did they appear? Before or after the abortion?" As I studied them one by one and searched my memory, each answer came back the same. There was no doubt that all of my problems had begun after my abortion.

My physical relationship with Joe had been normal before the abortion. I had been happy before and had never had the anxiety I had now lived with for years. Until the abortion I'd never experienced fear or panic attacks. I started wondering.

At the next volunteer training class, we watched a video called "Letters to my children." It was about a woman who had had four abortions and had achieved closure to her guilt, pain and sense of loss by writing letters to each of her lost babies. It was a very moving story with an uplifting theme of God's unconditional love and unlimited ability to forgive.

Everyone else's mascara was running down their faces and I still was feeling nothing! I thought to myself, "What is wrong with me?" Could I be so cold-hearted that I couldn't even cry? I felt absolutely nothing.

After class, once everyone else had left, the director gently nudged me to take the tape home and watch it with my husband, Joe. I thought, "OK, no big deal."

She said that watching the tape again would be sort of like homework for the telephone counseling I was training for. That made sense to me.

The next day was a Saturday and we were alone in the house, just Joe and I. Our sons had gone on a camping trip with the youth group of our church. We went to our business and did paperwork for most of the day. That whole day, I felt a mixed sense of trepidation and anticipation, like something important was about to happen to me, to us. When we got home I could bear it no longer. I told Joe about the tape and he agreed to watch it with me.

As the woman talked of her loss, described her tears of sorrow and the joy she now had because of the forgiveness and healing she had experienced, tears ran down her face. I almost sat upright as a thought so powerful and crystal clear struck through to the very core of my being. I had never been sorry! I had said I was sorry in my moments of desperation. I had called out to God in a "save me, take me away from all this" manner. Could it be that easy? Was that all I had to do all these years? Apologize and ask forgiveness? I didn't have to make it right or take it back? How could I have anyway!

As I was crying, I turned to see my husband crying as well. I had tried to cry many times through the years, but the few tears I'd cried were both frustrating and unsatisfying. The tears that poured out of me this day turned from purging and cleansing to hopeful and joyous! I asked for and received forgiveness from my husband and from God for taking into my hands a decision that was not mine to make. For the first time, in a long time, I really felt like I was going to be OK.

That day was October 14, 2000 and I celebrate it as my second birthday. Since then we have brought our secret sin out of the darkness and into His light. I am a prisoner of guilt and shame no longer. God has completely and totally healed me and all I had to do was ask Him.

He showed me where my wound had begun. It began twenty-four years ago in an abortion clinic in North Carolina.

My prayer and hope in telling my story is that should you experience these symptoms, these problems in your life, you will realize that you needn't suffer. God has been so generous and merciful to me and He will be to you as well.

The years ahead are exciting and promising. I thank God for where He has brought me. I thank Him for where He is taking me. Mostly, I thank Him for forgiving me and teaching me how to forgive myself and others.

My marriage has never been better. Our sexual relationship, as well as our emotional bond with one another, has been restored.

Due to my earlier fear of becoming pregnant again, Joe and I adopted our two wonderful boys who are the light of our lives. My husband was truly "heaven sent." He stood by me, loved me when I was pretty unlovable and never hesitated in his forgiveness. I will always have to live with what I did, but it will no longer steal the joy that I know God wants for me, my marriage and my family.

Trina

My story begins in November of 1982. I was fifteen years old. You could say I was an average and normal teenage girl. My teachers and parents would classify me as a good student. My grades were consistently As and Bs. Like most girls my age, I enjoyed meeting new people and participating in school activities in and out of the classroom.

My boyfriend was eighteen years old and we had been dating for a little over two years. During the beginning of our relationship, I protected my virginity. We fooled around a lot, but we refrained from sexual intercourse.

Two years into the relationship, however, I believed him when he said he would love me forever. I decided I didn't want to wait anymore. What was I waiting for anyway? I wanted to take our relationship "all the way." So, I offered him my virginity and he gladly accepted. And that's when our sexual relationship began.

One afternoon I was sitting in the living room talking with my stepsister. She had just found out that she was pregnant. We were discussing her plans when mom walked in, took one look at me and screamed angrily, "You're pregnant, too!" Shocked, I just sat there. I couldn't believe my ears. She must be crazy? How could she know just by looking at me that I was pregnant? I'd only been sexually active for a month! There was no way I could be pregnant! I couldn't remember when I'd had my last period so I wasn't able to answer her demanding questions. She immediately made an appointment for me to see our family doctor. He had been mom's doctor for years. He was the same doctor who had delivered me, and also my brothers.

This would be my first gynecological exam. The next day mom drove me to the doctor's office to confirm what she already knew. Mom waited in the lobby for me as the nurse took me back into the examining room.

As I lay there on the cold, hard table, I was very uncomfortable. I didn't even know these people. Besides the fact that I felt humiliated, the exam was basically non-eventful. After the exam, the nurse called for my mom. I listened as they were engrossed in a conversation about me and my situation. Mom's suspicions were confirmed. She was right and there was no doubt about it. I was pregnant. How did she know? They continued to speak about me as if I wasn't in the room. My presence wasn't acknowledged! Neither of them asked me what I might want to do. They decided the only option I had was abortion. Abortion! What were they talking about?

During this whole process, I'd assumed that if I was, in fact, pregnant, I would be able to keep my baby. No one was demanding that my stepsister had to have an abortion!

I'd never thought much about abortion before. It was so foreign to me. I can't say that I was pro-life or pro-choice. I never expected to be in a situation like the one I was in. But, what I did know, with every fiber of my being, was that I desperately wanted my baby. A force inside of me was screaming that abortion was wrong! Too bad, I was the only one who could hear it. No one was interested in my opinion anyway. That point was made perfectly clear.

Mom and the doctor had already determined that the "procedure" needed to take place right away. Not once, did they consult me. They only told me what was going to happen.

Before we left his office, I was scheduled for an immediate abortion. On the drive home, I begged mom to change her mind. I told her that abortion was like "throwing a baby in the trashcan." I couldn't stop crying. Yet, my cries were ignored and my efforts to sway her failed. Mom's mind was made up and no one or nothing was going to change it. I had never felt so helpless in my life. Mom said this would be our secret. She said my dad and brothers never needed to know.

The next day came quickly. Mom drove me to the hospital. When we arrived, I was instructed to undress and given a hospital gown to wear. The nurse came in and inserted an I.V. needle into my arm. This would carry the drug into my vein that would eventually put me to sleep. I lay there thinking, "What am I doing here? I want to get up and leave! Why can't I move? I never agreed to this!"

Next, they strapped my right and left arms onto the operating table and placed my feet in stirrups. A warm blanket was draped over me and I was beginning to feel drowsy. I noticed a machine in the room that looked peculiar with holes in it. I watched as the I.V. dripped the drugs slowly into my vein. The nurse told me it would be over soon. She said it wouldn't take longer than fifteen minutes. And that's the last thing I remember.

An hour and a half later, I woke up in a semi-private room. I was sharing it with a young woman. She was very sympathetic and told me how she had also miscarried a baby. I guess they hadn't told her the real reason I was there. I realized we weren't on the baby floor and so I asked her, "Why did they put us here instead of on the nursery floor?" She replied, "Oh my gosh, they would never do that to us. It would be too painful." That's when I was sure she didn't know. I thought about how different our situations were. Her loss was unexpected. Mine was planned.

The next day, Mom picked me up and took me home. We drove together in silence. Mom didn't ask any questions and I offered nothing in return. I quickly learned from her demeanor that this day was never to be mentioned again. I had been experiencing heavy cramping, but worse than that was the emptiness I felt inside. I didn't feel like a whole person anymore. It was as though a large chunk of my insides had been taken from me in a matter of a short fifteen minutes.

When we arrived home, everyone was going about normal activities. I sat in the living room listening to their various conversations. How could everyone just sit there and go on about their lives! Didn't they know what just happened to me! No, I remembered, they didn't. I couldn't stand it anymore.

My bedroom was downstairs in our finished basement. I slowly got up and exited the room. No one even noticed. I retreated in my bedroom for the rest of the day and night. I cried myself to sleep and when I woke up the next morning, I cried some more. My mother never came downstairs to check on me. I suppose she could have while I was sleeping. She never questioned me as to how I was doing. No one understood why I was so upset. Mom's attitude was "It's done, forget about it." I wish she could have showed me how to do that. To this day, I've never been able to forget about it.

Within a short time, my grades dropped drastically. I stopped participating in class like I had used to. The teacher's assumed I was going through some type of teenage depression, but they never asked what was going on with me. I wouldn't have told them anyway. No one could ever know what I'd done. During classes, I would turn my desk towards the wall. This gave me the sense of being alone. I didn't want to have to look at anyone and I sure didn't want anyone looking at me. I was so afraid that they would know, that somehow they could tell. I'd never had a failing grade throughout my school years, yet now I had several.

Seclusion from everyone and everything became my only sanctuary. The more secluded I was, the better I felt. I continued to see my boyfriend, but he offered no substitute for my solitude. Depression was becoming my normal way of life. Feelings of hopelessness became my constant companion. I don't think mom noticed I was quickly falling into a deep pit with no way out. I was screaming, "Help me!" But, again, no one was listening.

Mom assumed since she had let it alone that I had too. She thought that I'd forgotten about it by now. Looking back, no one had paid attention to what was happening to me. Not my teachers or my family.

Six months after my abortion, I made a decision to end my life. I showed my stepsister the drug of my choice and told her I was going to take them. She said, "No you're not, you're crazy!" I walked away from her, twenty pills in hand, and walked downstairs to my bedroom. I swallowed all of them at once. I laid down on my bed and waited. I wanted so badly for it to be over. I hoped it would happen quickly. I desperately had to get out of the living hell that I'd been living in for too long. I prayed and hoped it would happen quickly.

My stepsister must have noticed the serious look on my face because soon after, she came downstairs and asked me, "Did you take those pills?" I answered yes and lay back down." Mom came down. She walked over to me and slapped me hard on the face. She yelled, "If you want to do that, then go ahead and do it!"

Mom ran upstairs and immediately called an ambulance. I was rushed to the hospital to have my stomach pumped. In the emergency room, my mother continued to berate me for what I'd done. She was convinced that I did this to get back at her. To this day, I deny that accusation. I just wanted my life to end. I wanted the pain to stop. It was a constant ache that wouldn't go away and I just wanted it to be over. Couldn't anybody understand that?

My father came to the emergency room. He's always shown me love by buying me beautiful gifts. Dad never asked me why I did it. He only wanted to know what I wanted him to get me. I told him I wanted a bright, shiny red robe. A few hours later, on his way to work, he showed up with a large bag. In it was the most beautiful red robe I'd ever seen. As wonderful as his gift was, I still felt empty inside.

I was placed on the psychiatric ward where I was to remain for the next thirty days. The counselors tried to involve me in group sessions, but I wanted nothing to do with them. I continued to search for places where I could be alone. It wasn't easy. They were constantly watching me. I started crocheting all day long, even during the counseling sessions. Some of the other patients would ask, "Why does she keep shaking her leg?" The doctors would respond that I was just nervous. The doctors were never told that I'd had an abortion. And they never thought to ask. My mother wasn't going to tell them and neither was I.

After thirty days on the psychiatric ward, I was released to go home. Mom picked me up and again we drove in silence. We never have, to this day, talked about that month in the hospital. The subject of my failed suicide attempt was never brought up again.

I tried to do better when I reentered school, but I rarely talked to anyone and was still separating myself from everyone. When the school year ended, one of my teachers made a comment that I've never forgotten. She said, "I would like Trina to stand up. Class, I want you to give her a round of applause because I didn't think she was going to make it through this year. Trina, welcome back to society." The class roared with applause. I can remember thinking, "If you only knew."

After the abortion, mom insisted that I be put on birth control pills. I continued to date the father of my aborted baby and we were still involved sexually. The relationship wasn't good for me, but I was too weak to get out of it. Two years had passed. It was now 1984. I was eighteen years old and a senior in high school and I was pregnant again. I knew I needed to tell my mother. She was in the bathroom getting ready to go out. I walked in, slid down the wall and sat on the floor. "Mom, I'm pregnant." She said, "Well, this is your last year of high school. All I ask of you is that you graduate." And that was that. No talk of abortion, no yelling, no screaming. Nothing. She just wanted me to graduate.

There was no emotion in my boyfriend's voice when I told him I was pregnant again. He wasn't a source of support or encouragement. No one could stop me. I was having this baby. I stayed in school until the last two months before graduation. It was then that I started going to the Mommy/Baby School. On graduation night, I was six months pregnant.

Three months later, I gave birth to a beautiful baby girl and she and I moved into our own apartment. I continued to see her father and at times you could say we were living together. Two years later, in 1986, I was pregnant again. This time, he was furious. He made it clear right away that he didn't want any more children. He said this time it was my problem to deal with all by myself. Like he'd been there before?

I decided on my own to have my second abortion. I didn't see any other way. I told no one about my decision. I asked a girlfriend to give me a ride to the hospital for some "minor surgery" that I needed. She agreed to drive me and waited until I was finished. The same doctor who delivered me and performed my first abortion would also perform my second one. It was almost exactly the same as the first time. I was put to sleep again and woke up an hour later. But this time, I knew there was only one person I could blame for what I'd done and that person was me. I never told her or anyone else the real reason that I went to the hospital that day.

When it was over, I was taken by elevator to the recovery room where I would spend the next hour before my release from the hospital. I was crying uncontrollably on the ride down. There was a nurse on the elevator with me. She said, "It's going to be OK." I told her, "You don't know what I've just done, you don't understand." I repeated this over and over. She never knew what I was talking about.

Why don't we learn from the past? I should have known better. Instantly, I regretted my decision, but it was too late. My baby was gone now, thrown in some garbage can. How ironic is that. The words I had spoken to my mother were now haunting me.

Over the years, I wasn't able to develop friendships with women so I didn't have many friends. I always backed away from any relationships getting too close. It was safer for me to isolate myself from everyone. This way, I would never have to share any of my secrets. I was convinced that if these women knew what I'd done, they'd want nothing to do with me. So, I isolated myself from any friendships that might threaten me.

I continued to fall into deep depression. And at times, I would experience fits of rage that I didn't quite understand. The smallest things could set me off. I wasn't sure if they were coming from my abortion experiences or not. I just assumed that I should be over them by now.

The relationship with my boyfriend was going nowhere. Finally, I mustered every ounce of courage I had and ended my relationship with him. It was harder than I thought it would be, but I did it. A year later, I would meet the man who would be my future husband. I didn't tell him about my abortions until four years into our marriage. I don't know what I was afraid of because when I did tell him, he was a wonderful source of support to me. He never condemned or judged me. We would later become the parents of two more beautiful daughters.

Through the years, I'd never dealt with the "flaws" in my character. I accepted them as a part of my make-up. In early 2000, I was in my car listening to a Christian Radio Station. A woman was sharing her testimony of how an abortion she'd had years earlier had affected her life. She talked about the ways she had been feeling and shared how God had healed her. She was talking about me! I could relate to everything she said. I couldn't get out of my car. I was riveted by every word she said. Her name was Sherry Brown. At the end of her testimony, she gave a plea for anyone interested in becoming a volunteer counselor at the Crisis Pregnancy Center to please call and reserve your spot for the classes that would begin soon.

I called right away. I signed up and began attending the classes. I desperately felt this need to help other women. During one of our training classes, some women came in. They had just returned from Russia where they'd been conducting Post-Abortion Recovery Classes for Russian women. I later found that women from all over the world who had had abortions were experiencing the same types of problems I was.

A woman from the group asked us, "Has any one of you ever had an abortion?" One woman stood up. It wasn't me. She went on to say that they would be starting another training class for any of us interested in counseling post-abortive women. Although, I didn't share my secret at this time, I immediately volunteered for the classes.

I soon found myself, along with several other women, attending the Post-Abortion Recovery Training Classes. During the first class, we were each asked why we were participating. I answered, "Well, I heard this woman talking about how she had an abortion years ago and how God had healed her. She was on the radio."

A woman in the group began to cry. She said, "I'm that woman. I'm Sherry Brown. I didn't think anyone was listening that night. That was the first time I'd shared my testimony and I thought I had failed miserably."

I said, "No, Sherry, it's because of what you shared that I'm here. It's because of you." I would later confess my abortion experiences with these precious women and that first confession began my path to complete healing. The truth truly does set you free.

I am now a Post-Abortive Recovery Counselor in Greenville, South Carolina. I am so humbled that the Lord can and does use me the way He does to help other women who have experienced the traumatic effects of abortion. God has totally healed me and is restoring joy in my life that I haven't experienced in many years. I am so proud to serve a God like Him! And I will serve Him for the rest of my life!

As the reader of this story, you may find it hard to believe what I'm about to tell you. The relationship I share with my mother is an unusual one. We are closer than any two people could be. Our relationship is one of the most precious things in my life and I cherish it. She is literally my best friend. She is my confidante. We live in different states, but we speak several times a day by phone. I don't know what I'd do without her.

The Lord protected my heart from feeling bitterness or anger towards her all through the years. Never once, even when I was fifteen years old, did I hate or blame my mother. I have never blamed my mother. She has always loved me unconditionally. My mother thought she was doing what was best for me that day so long ago. All mothers want to protect their children and my mother is no different. I wouldn't trade her for anyone. She has helped me with the struggles that I've faced in my life. She has stuck by me through thick and thin. I can't imagine what it must be like for her to now know the kind of pain I was going through. We've both experienced tremendous guilt for what happened. But, thank God, we are strong in our faith and we know that we serve a God who has totally forgiven us. The Lord has also helped me to forgive everyone involved with my abortion, including the doctor.

I love and cherish my mother. I wanted to make sure that you knew that. I make sure she knows it everyday.

Rachel

I believed him. He was, or so I thought, the answer to my prayers. I had never felt before what I felt for him and I hung on every word he said. When our relationship was good, you couldn't have found a better one. But when it was bad, I had to be careful about what I did or anything I said for fear of what he might do to me.

We had been living together for nearly two years when he came home one day and announced that it was over. Just like that. He needed "space" and wanted out. I begged him to reconsider. I did everything I could think of to persuade him that we belonged together. I made his favorite meals, made sure I looked as beautiful as I could and even seduced him every chance I got to show him how good we were together. Nothing worked. He never turned the sex down, but he still left every morning.

A few weeks passed and I realized I'd missed my period. I was so excited. I missed him so much and just knew this pregnancy was the answer to my prayers. I didn't do it on purpose. We were using protection so he couldn't accuse me of trapping him.

When I called to tell him my pregnancy test was positive, I didn't get the reaction I'd hoped for. He didn't believe me. He called me a liar, among other things and said he wanted proof that I was really pregnant. I couldn't believe it! This man of my dreams was turning into a nightmare! He said he loved me, he promised to grow old with me and never leave me. He was the liar, not me!

I was ripped apart. I didn't want to live anymore. How could this man I loved so much it hurt be treating me this way? I forced myself not to talk to him for a few days and then the phone rang. It was him. He wanted to know if I had his "proof" yet. I told him I would gladly go to the doctor with him to take another test. I offered to pee right in front of him! He declined. He continued to tell me that I was using this to get him back and that it wasn't working. I thought I was going to die. I'd never experienced such pain in my life.

Two weeks later, I made what I felt was the only decision I could. A decision that would forever haunt me. I didn't want to. The thought of having an abortion was killing me, but I felt pushed in a corner. What else was I supposed to do? My girlfriend begged me to go through with the pregnancy. She said she would adopt my baby. I said, "I can't carry a baby for nine months and then give my baby away!" There was no way I could do that. So, instead I decided to kill my baby! What sense does that make? I was so blind.

I kept going back and forth with my decision. Evil won out so on a Tuesday morning, I drove myself to the local abortion clinic. I gave my money and was escorted down the hallway to an examining room. While I was standing there, a nurse asked my name. When I told her, she said there was a phone call for me. I couldn't believe it. Could it be him? Was he calling to stop me? It had to be him! My prayers had been answered!

But it wasn't him. It was my girlfriends. They wanted to ask me again if I was sure this was what I wanted to do. I wasn't sure, but I answered yes anyway. Maybe if I said it enough, I could convince myself that this was the right thing to do.

But how could I have answered yes? That was the farthest thing from the truth. One thing that I knew was that I was sure I didn't want to do this. But I did it anyway. Why? Why?

I was then taken into the room where the "procedure" would take place. Physically, it was relatively painless, like an annual pap smear. But, I thought the pain in my heart would surely kill me. You might be thinking, if that were true, how could you go through with it? I can't answer that. Some force kept me on that table and wouldn't let me get up, even though I wanted to. I wanted to be anywhere else, but I literally couldn't move.

When it was over, one of my girlfriends picked me up. I cried in her arms and she comforted me. She assured me that she still loved me. She said everything was going to be all right. She dropped me off at my apartment. She offered to come in, but I told her I wanted to be alone. Alone with the realization of what I'd just done. I sobbed and begged for God's mercy. I tried to sleep, but I couldn't.

A few hours later, my phone rang. My boyfriend was calling from out of town and he wanted me to see him. He would be flying in the next day and said, "I've been thinking about things. I don't want you to do anything. We can do this. I'm sorry and I want to marry you and have our baby."

Oh, so now it was our baby! I said, "You're too late. It's over. I never want to see you again. Just leave me alone."

At the writing of this story, thirteen long years have passed since my abortion. I have and will suffer for that decision for the remainder of my life. I can't look at a pregnant woman without thinking about the abortion. I wonder what he would have looked like. I wonder what kind of person he would have been. These thoughts will forever be in the back of my mind, no matter how hard I try to erase them.

Abortion is not only deadly to an innocent child, it is devastating to the mother who chooses it. By the grace of God, I found out about help for women like me. It's a post-abortion recovery retreat called, "Forgiven and Set Free." Through this Bible study, I found true and complete healing in Jesus Christ for my abortion. If it weren't for God, I don't know if I would still be alive today.

Many times since my abortion, I've wanted to take my own life. The guilt of being alive was sometimes hard to live with. With the Lord's help, I've learned to live with what I've done, but I will never be completely over it.

I am now married to an incredible man who treats me like I'm the most wonderful woman in the world. He tells me often that I'm the best thing that's ever happened to him. He constantly reminds me of how special I am to him. He compliments me frequently, but it's sometimes hard for me to receive his adoration.

During my marriage, I've suffered two miscarriages. This is another common result from having an abortion. Sex isn't as pleasurable to me as it once was, but God is helping me restore that area of my life. I thank God for a patient husband!

What kind of a woman has an abortion? What kind of a mother could kill her own baby? Abortion does not discriminate. Just as I was blind to the truth of what my decision would cost me, I was blind to the truth that I was carrying a real, live baby.

No one at the clinic ever told me I could experience the grief that I've had for years. They made it seem so simple and easy. They lied to me. They lie to women everyday.

I'm not in denial anymore. My baby is gone. He's in Heaven with God and I will forever miss him. I loved him too late. I will forever regret that I didn't allow myself to be his mother. I wonder what he would have looked like or what sports he may have played. I think about talking to him about girls and love.

One day I know I will see him and when I do, I will ask for his forgiveness. I will tell him that I loved his father too much.

My baby is gone, but I'm still here. And I plan to make the best of my time. I want to warn women everywhere that abortion is murder. We were created to give life, not take it. When you do something against your human nature, you'll pay a high price. One I hope more and more women will choose not to pay.

Yes, the children of aborted women are victims. We, the mothers of those children, are the other victims. Someone should have told me the truth. Since they didn't, I will.

About the Author

Victoria Laktash is a wife, mother, grandmother, non-profit executive and professional speaker. She's spoken to thousands of men, women and children all over the world.

Victoria has been highly successful in shifting the attitudes of young people regarding the positives of making healthy choices by practicing abstinence from alcohol, drugs, tobacco, gang activity and sex before marriage.

As a self-proclaimed risk taker, Victoria is bold when delivering her messages. Her message "Real Love Waits, I don't Until I Do" will keep the listener on the edge of their seat.

Victoria has worked as a post abortion counselor with pregnancy centers and churches for over 15 years. Her "Breaking Free From Your Past and Getting Real With God" message is one that every person should hear.

For booking and scheduling information, you can contact Victoria directly at www.VictoriaLaktash.com or email Gloria Leyda at info@AmbassadorSpeakers.com

If you would like to submit your story about an abortion experience or past regret to be considered for Victoria's next book, please email your story and contact information to VLaktash@gmail.com

11290968R00039

Made in the USA
Charleston, SC
13 February 2012